8/06

SO-EBU-573

Heads Up!

There are lots of extras in this book aimed at helping you with creating your own blogs and ezines.

How To Use This Book

BRAIN JAM

Brain Jams offer activities to get you thinking creatively and give you a chance to hone your skills.

★ PROJECT JUMP START

Project Jump Starts provide that sometimes necessary extra push to get you going on your own blog or ezine.

TIP FILE

Tip Files offer up all sorts of helpful suggestions and hints on getting the project done.

RESOURCES   RESOURCES

One of these icons will lead you to more information.

ORDINARY   **EXTRAORDINARY**

Throughout the book you will see the ordinary and the extraordinary side by side. With revisions and some thought, these comparisons show you what you can accomplish.

For Ronald Breininger

Photographs © 2006: Corbis Images: 86 (Steve Kaufman), 89 (José Fuste Raga/zefa), 103 (Bettmann).

Cover design: Marie O'Neill
Series design: Simon Says Design! and Marie O'Neill
Art production: The Design Lab
Cover and interior illustrations by Kevin Pope

Library of Congress Cataloging-in-Publication Data

Rominger, Lynne.
  Extraordinary blogs and ezines / by Lynne Rominger.
    p. cm. — (F.W. prep)
  Includes bibliographical references and index.
  ISBN 0-531-16765-8 (lib. bdg.)   0-531-13904-2 (pbk.)
  1. Weblogs. 2. Electronic journals. I. Title. II. Series.
  TK5105.8884.R66 2006
  006.7—dc22   2005021666

EXTRAORDINARY
Blogs and Ezines

by Lynne Rominger

Franklin Watts®

A Division of Scholastic Inc.
New York • Toronto • London • Auckland • Sydney
Mexico City • New Delhi • Hong Kong
Danbury, Connecticut

EXTRAORDINARY BLOGS AND EZINES

ASSIGNMENT: BLOGS AND EZINES 6

You have been given an assignment—create a blog or an ezine. Find out why your teacher thinks this is a good idea.

Why Should I Use This Book? 10

Blogs and ezines are everywhere these days. Mastering the skills necessary to create them may be one of the cornerstones of your future success.

THE ONLINE COMMUNICATION PROCESS ~~OUTLINED~~ *Unplugged*

1 YOU'VE GOT BLOG:
Speak Up, Speak Out! 13

Wondering exactly what makes a blog and how it is different from instant messages and e-mail? Read on to find out.

2 BUILD IT AND THEY WILL COME:
How to Create a Weblog 33

This is where we get down to the nitty-gritty of writing your blog and getting it online.

3 STYLE AND FORM:
The Electronic Magazine 55

What makes an ezine different from a print magazine? How is it different from any other Web site? Find the answers to these questions and more in this chapter.

4 GO EZINE, ACTIVATE
How to Publish an Ezine 65

Need to know how to create a Web site and get your ezine up and running? Look no further.

HOW-TO MINI-GUIDES

5 READY, SET, BLOG!:
Projects to Get You Rave Reviews from Your Teachers   79

Stuck for ideas? Look here for projects on lots of different
subjects, with helpful hints on making yours stand out from
the crowd.

6 EZINES:
Hitting Newsstands Now   109

Need some ideas for your ezine assignment? Here are a few to
get you started.

THE BACK MATTER

To Find Out More:
Need a little extra help? Turn here.   122

Index:
Want to find something fast?
This is the place to go.   125

About the Author:
Curious about who put this all together?   128

ASSIGNMENT:

So why have you been assigned blogs and ezines in your classes?After all, how many hours do you spend on the computer instant messaging (IM'ing), accessing information of interest, downloading programs and pictures, shopping, researching topics for classes, and writing e-mail? Chances are that you log on at least once a day for several minutes to an hour or more. In many ways, the students of today are far more comfortable with, and knowledgeable about, the Internet than most educators.

Creating blogs and ezines helps fulfill the plan your state has for your education. Each state in the country has its own educational curriculum plan for its students. These plans are called educational standards. From **Connecticut** to **Idaho**, from **Minnesota** to **South Carolina**, the standards call for students to tackle a variety of technology-based projects. In Connecticut, for instance, students are expected to use technology to gather, synthesize, organize, and spread information. Educators in South Carolina want students to be able to use the Internet to communicate with others.

Blogs and Ezines

Even if state standards didn't require you to create Web-based projects, doesn't it make assignments much more fun if you can let your creative energies and Internet interest drive your project? The more fun you have with an assignment—from trigonometry to journalism to biology—the better you'll retain the information.

So see, you're not alone. Thousands of other students are tackling the same types of assignments this year. The trick is to make your blog or ezine catch your teacher's attention. How can you give your project a twist that makes it distinct from all the others? In a word, how do you make it EXTRAORDINARY?

Part of making any project extraordinary—whether it's a blog, an ezine, or some other type of project—is knowing what is expected of you and surpassing those expectations. These assignments are opportunities for you to develop and express your own creative ideas—and to develop your skills as a writer and communicator.

Blogs are flying across the nation and ezines are eXpected in inboXes everywhere.

Check Out Your State's Standards!

One way to stay ahead of the game is to take a look at your state's standards for this year and the years ahead. If you're ready to look into your future, try visiting the Developing Educational Standards site at: **http://www.edstandards.org/Standards.html.** There you can find links to the educational departments of every state and even focus on language arts in particular.

For more of a national overview of language arts standards, let's take a look at a few of the twelve national educational standards created by the National Council of Teachers of English (NCTE). (For a complete list, visit NCTE's Web site, **http://www.ncte.org.**)

By creating extraordinary blogs and ezines, you can demonstrate your mastery of several key skills mentioned in the standards:

- An extraordinary blog or ezine shows that you can use written and visual language for learning, enjoyment, persuasion, and exchanging information.

- Creating an extraordinary blog or ezine demonstrates that you know how to use a variety of technological and information resources—such as databases, computer networks, and video—to gather and synthesize information and communicate your knowledge.

- Blogging and creating ezines allow you to participate as a knowledgeable, reflective, creative, and critical member of various literary communities.

Heads Up!

Before thinking outside of the box, you've got to know what's inside the box—the assignment—and what the teacher expects of you. Many teachers grade according to whether or not you included all of the components they wanted you to include in your assignment. Although your teacher may give you specific grading rules in advance, not all do. These rules are often known as a rubric, and while some teachers swear by them, others do not use them at all. But you can be sure of getting the grade you want by critically reading your assignment sheet.

Look over what the teacher expects to see in your weblog or ezine. For example, are you expected to post a paragraph that details a current event each day and elicit at least five other student responses? Are you required to change three content items on your ezine weekly? The best thing to do is to make notes of the items your teacher lists as part of the assignment. From there, start thinking out of the box as to how you'll present it!

Why Should I Use This Book?

Believe it or not, there used to be a time when very few people had computers in their homes. All libraries had files called card catalogs. Long, skinny drawers were stuffed full of cards. Each card held all the information about one book. You had to thumb through the cards to find what you needed. Homework was written out by hand or typed on a typewriter.

Today, things are different. Much of the information in the world is at your fingertips. Just type a few words in a search engine and get:

1 The latest news about your favorite basketball team

2 A new recipe to try out on your family

3 Breaking news from around the world

4 Just about any other piece of information you can think of!

The passing of information and dissemination of important news that used to take hours, days, or even weeks now happens almost instantaneously. Numerous Web sites, weblogs (blogs), and electronic magazines (ezines) help keep the information flowing.

In this book you will:

1 Learn exactly what weblogs and ezines are (that is, if you don't already know)

2 Discover what makes weblogs and ezines different from old-fashioned face-to-face conversations and printed magazines

Reading this book will also help you polish your:

1 Writing skills

2 Research skills

3 Web skills

Why does this matter? **Because most jobs require good writing skills, and an increasing number of jobs require excellent Internet and Web skills, too.** This book will help you fine-tune those skills. Soon you'll be blogging and creating ezines like a pro—impressing your teachers as they grade your extraordinary project and, just maybe, helping you impress potential employers sometime in the not-too-distant future.

So read on to find out how easy it is to create your own blogs and Web pages. Instead of living through the monotony of another essay, **keep turning these pages to learn how to write, create, showcase, and deliver your ingenious thoughts and ideas on a variety of subjects**—all with the possibility of an audience in the millions! Who knows? One of your assignments from this book may bring you international Internet superstardom.

weblog

Internet

personal blog

conversation

Internet

To

politic

weblog

w

12

online journa

YOU'VE GOT BLOG

Speak Up, Speak Out!

Speak Up, Speak Out!

On the Internet, everyone online gets to have a voice. Where once writers scribbled their thoughts in diaries or journals—very few of which were ever published—today the Internet gives us all an unprecedented opportunity to speak up and speak out!

A weblog is an online journal with entries from its creator. The creator also gives readers and invited guests the chance to respond. That makes a weblog an **active, dated conversation on a variety of topics,** usually with a single theme. The blogs out there range from the day-to-day life and interests of teens to professionally created political forums where people debate current policies.

No topic is untouched by weblogs. Scan the Internet, and you'll find people posting their ideas about everything from aging to agnosticism, from sports to choosing a university, from fashion to religious fanaticism. Although a blog may simply showcase the thoughts of the blogger, some of the best engage their readers and guest bloggers with thoughtful discourse and compelling conversation. You can learn a lot of interesting (and helpful!) information on blogs.

Heads Up!

Check it out!

If you don't have a clue as to what a weblog looks like or you need creative help, try checking out blogs that interest you. Go to **http://www.google.com** and type in "blog" and one of your interests. Do you like music? Type "music." Sports? Type "sports." Then spend some time looking at all the different ways people blog. This activity should help you come up with some ideas for your own blog.

Need more help searching for blogs to look at? Here are the best resources to consult before you go hunting:

http://blogpulse.com

http://blogsearch.google.com

http://icerocket.com/

http://search.yahoo.com (combines blogs and news)

http://www.technorati.com (most popular and established)

A Blog Is Born

Blogging is generally regarded to have entered our mainstream culture in about 1997. But it was only after the terrorist attacks on the United States on September 11, 2001, that blogging came into its own as a valid and invigorating way to communicate. After the attacks, bloggers flocked to sites to discuss the war on terrorism. In the article "Online Uprising," Catherine Seipp wrote, "In general, 'blog' used to mean a personal online diary, typically concerned with boyfriend problems or techie news. But after September 11, a slew of new or refocused media junkie/political sites reshaped the entire Internet media landscape. Blog now refers to a Web journal that comments on the news—often by criticizing the media and usually in rudely clever tones—with links to stories that back up the commentary with evidence." Meanwhile, people who had never done so before hit blogs hard, searching for answers and information. Many new blogs sprouted within this political climate. Soon, respected organizations such as MSNBC and the San Jose *Mercury News* hired staffers to write weblogs, turning the underground blogging scene into mainstream news.

Today, **blogging is widespread**. Universities offer weblog classes. Along with e-mail and instant messaging, blogging has become an integral part of our communication with each other.

Blog Make and Model

Generally speaking, blogs are either personal or topical.

Personal Blogs

- **Online diaries** or journals that include the daily life and events of the writers

- Typically other **bloggers** who post on the site **are friends**.

- **Discussions are personal** among those in the clique.

Topical Blogs

- Consider a **specific subject**

- All posts focus on the dissemination of information.

- **Discussions are subject based.** Siamese cats, flying saucers, silly hats, Transylvania castles—all are possible topics. Have a specific interest? The topical blog exists for you.

Your assignments will be topical in nature. Your instructor, for example, may ask you to blog about a specific novel, such as *Of Mice and Men* by **John Steinbeck**; a current event, such as an election; or a biological process, photosynthesis for example.

About my blog . . .

Heads Up!

So Here's the Scoop

Is blog a noun or a verb? The answer: **Both!** It can be used in several grammatically correct ways, so let's take a look at each one. In 2004, dictionary publisher Merriam-Webster declared "blog" the Word of the Year. Blog is a noun meaning an online weblog. "Blogger" is another noun which means anyone who creates or contributes to a blog. "Blogging" is a verb for the action of creating or contributing to a blog.

Here are a few sentences to put the word in context: Jack spent two hours last night blogging. First, he had to answer a homework question about DNA on his biology teacher's blog. Later, he navigated to his best friend's blog on guitars, where a few of the bloggers (who also happen to be in his friend's band) posted their perspectives on the best guitars on the market.

A Blog by Any Other Name Would Sound As Sweet

Soon you will begin working on an assignment to create your own weblog. You may be worried about the technical aspects of the assignment. Sure, you can send an instant message (IM), but create a weblog from nothing? Chillax. **You'll find a list of easy blogging software leads and how-tos in the next chapter.** There may even be a software program that is compatible with the assignment and the World Wide Web access your teacher prefers.

Even though you'll be creating a blog for a class assignment, you just might find that you would like to create a private weblog for your own use. Think of how cool it would be to have a site created by you that covers all that you find amazing or crazy, and that people from around the globe (or a private group of members you let in) can visit and react to. **A weblog gives you a worldwide stage for sharing information as well as your individuality.**

Some of you may be thinking, "If it's only for my friends, why not just use instant messaging? Doesn't it do the same thing?" **Let's take a look at the differences between IM'ing and blogging.**

I M Out of Here!

Weblogs are unique compared to most forms of communication on the Internet. You may be scratching your head and thinking, "And more work, too." Not really. A blog may allow you to get your point across or share information in less time than it would if you instant messaged or e-mailed someone.

Instant messaging has become as popular with today's teens and young adults as the telephone was back when your parents were your age.

Instant messages

- are great for private conversations,

- are "in the moment" and usually not recorded,

- disappear when your conversation is over and you close the window.

> cindyloo: how r u doing jack?
>
> jack87: fine. did you do the take home test yet?
>
> cindyloo: nope, but, i did my homework for tomorrow.
>
> jack87: cool, want to help me with mine?

A blog, on the other hand, lets you state your case in one place, known as a permalink. A permalink is the permanent address of your blog. Blogs provide you the opportunity to save information you may want or need later. They let you keep a running log.

Remember the guitar blog we mentioned earlier? Let's say that all the bloggers start posting about great guitarists in history, and soon Jerry Horton of Papa Roach is mentioned, along with his contributions to the lyrics of the band's socially charged songs. What if your teacher assigns a research paper on the social or political commentary found in modern music? If all of the people who had been blogging had been instant messaging instead, all the notes on Jerry Horton would be—poof!—gone.

With the guitar blog, however, you can:

- access the dated archive,

- find the information.

Voila! Your paper is being written with just a few keystrokes!

Blogs provide the ability to post links that are retained within the blog. If, during the guitar postings, someone posted links showcasing bands that devoted their lyrics to social consciousness, you've got another lead. With instant messaging, the chances of moving to and from links during the conversation are limited and certainly not permanent.

TIP FILE

All weblogs and blog-related Web sites are referred to as the **blogosphere**. When a topic emerges or erupts all over many blogs, it's referred to as a **blogstorm**.

Try This

There aren't many teens today who haven't instant messaged their friends. In many ways, a blog is just a permanent IM, so don't feel intimidated by blogging. Try this: IM a friend and ask that friend to carry on a conversation about an event in the news or a subject of interest to both of you. Maybe there is a big controversy at school about inappropriate dancing at homecoming. Ask how your friend feels about the school administration's rules about dances. Print out your IM after you have chatted for about fifteen minutes on the subject. Voilà! You just created a miniblog—but without the permanency.

Remember, an IM gets "erased" when you shut down the window, but a blog is still out there, just like a publication.

You Did Not Just Write That! Examining Blogs Critically

Before we go any further, let's see if you and a few friends can find three blogs and review them critically. Here's the drill:

1 In groups of three, come up with three topics that you all think are interesting or would be of interest to most people. For this assignment, celebrities and specific bands, groups, or performers are off-limits. You're looking for topical blogs.

2 Go online and search for blogs in the categories you've chosen.

3 Print out a few pages of the blogs you find.

4 For each blog, discuss the questions below. Write short answers down to share with your teacher and the class.

Questions:

- What is the theme of the blog? Hint: Does it cover a particular interest or does it dissolve into a free-for-all?

- Read over the blog entries. What entries provide good insight to the topic at hand? Highlight the entries and tell why you think they were thoughtful responses.

- What would you change about each blog to make it more helpful or interesting?

- Would any member of your group return to the blogs and post something? Why or why not? What would you post?

Congratulations!

You just critically examined a published work. When it comes time for your assignment, keep these questions in mind for your own weblog. Critically read what you write before you post it, and think about the bloggers reading and contributing to your weblog, in other words, your audience.

CELEBRITY SITES

Did you know that many of your favorite celebrities and athletes with Web sites also have blogging forums? Want to chat with Mia Tyler about her appearance in a VH1 reality show or her struggles with weight? Visit **http://www.miatyleronline.com** and blog away with the plus-size supermodel and daughter of Aerosmith's Steven Tyler about everything from guitar riffs to fashion. Navigate around to any and all of your favorite performers' official Web sites and see if they, too, are blogging.

Isn't This All Just a Journal or Diary?

Not really. In theory, diaries are personal. You don't necessarily want the world to read your innermost thoughts. After all, some arguments and hurt feelings can result if you aren't careful. What you write in a journal is considered to be for your eyes only. Blogs, on the other hand, let you express certain thoughts and interests publicly, as well as pass on useful information and conversation to others.

Let's look at the difference:

DIARY/JOURNAL:

> Mrs. Connors did it to me again today! She made me stand up and read my essay in class. I told her I hated that. I could just scream. Doesn't she ever listen to me? She's too old and deaf, I guess. We are discussing the war in Iraq and everyone has such heated opinions about it. I knew that George was going to jump all over me about what I said. After class, he was waiting for me. He drives me nuts.

BLOG:

> Today I had to read my essay about the war in Iraq aloud in class. I don't like doing that. It is embarrassing and people have a lot of emotional reactions to the topic. I don't like being confronted about my opinions.

Think of a **weblog** as the same thing as going out for coffee with your friends, but with permanence. Haven't you ever gotten into a deep conversation about something important going on in your school, city, family, or world and had a blast discussing the issue at hand? It's not exactly diary information, but your **personal perspectives and ideas** instead.

A weblog allows you to:

- have conversations,
- archive them for future reference.

If you like writing in a diary, you may love blogging.

HIT THE BOOKS

Think blogging sounds like something you could really get into? Bloggers have an extensive communication system built on acronyms and abbreviations—even more so than what you might find in e-mail or an IM. A great book to set you on the blogging path and provide you with an index of bloggers' acronyms and abbreviations is *Blogging for Teens* by John W. Gosney (Thompson Course Technology, 2004). This book is for the serious wannabe blogger and even shows you how to program your own blog.

Get a Load of Those Pipes— Finding Your Blog Voice

Before you even know the blog topic, your first step is to find your own blog voice. Part of the way you discover this is to read other blogs of interest to you. The tones of blogs differ greatly, depending on the writers and topics. As you can imagine, the blog of a seventeen-year-old girl who is ruminating on her life for her friends will sound vastly different from a journalist's blog that discusses breaking political news. A blog devoted to classical music will certainly sound different from a hip-hop blog. **Depending on the blog you begin or are assigned, you will want to find your voice and make sure it is appropriate for the topic.** While it is fine to use abbreviations in a personal blog meant for you and your friends, you will want to avoid blogging acronyms in assignments in which your instructor has asked you to discuss a topic, such as the causes of the Civil War.

Let's Talk About Me (Discovering Your Own Interests)

You probably have a good idea of your likes and dislikes—but have you ever put them down on paper? Right now, take out a piece of blank paper and answer these questions or fill in the blanks:

When I'm online, I like to read about _____ _____.

Most of the books in my room are about _____ _____.

When I talk to my friends, we discuss _____
_____.

The thing I am most passionate about is _____
_____.

In college, I hope to study _____
_____.

My favorite subject in school is _____
_____.

My hobbies off-campus include _____
_____.

The most important person in my life is _____,
because he/she _____.

A secret career desire of mine is _____
_____.

The best moment of my life happened when _____
_____.

When I pick up a newspaper, the section I go to
first is _____
_____.

Magazines I read are _____
_____.

If I already blog, the sites I go to most often are
about _____
_____.

Look over your answers. Based upon your
responses, if you were to create a blog of your
own interest, what would it be?

When answering questions, go for extraordinary answers. Really think about your responses. It will help you in the creation of your weblogs (and ezines, too).

QUESTION	ORDINARY	EXTRAORDINARY
What do you read about online?	Sports stuff	How to improve my soccer kicks and be a better right forward for my team.
What do you hope to study in college?	Science, with a focus on marine biology	Marine biology because I feel most at home when I am at the ocean.
What kind of books are in your room?	Horror and mystery books, *Analog* and *Skeptic*	I love anything that keeps me guessing or has a surprise ending, whether it is a mystery, horror story, or science fiction.
What topics get you upset, delighted, frustrated, or passionate?	Women's issues and child abuse	I am passionate about protecting the rights of people who often have had their rights completely ignored or overlooked.

Did you notice something about the extraordinary answers? They are **more specific** and **tell the reader more about you**.

PROJECT JUMP START

What's your favorite blog? Jot down three of your favorite places on the Web to chat, blog, or read what others have written. List the title of each blog and three reasons why you like it. Knowing what it is that interests you about someone else's blog may make it easier to get going on your own.

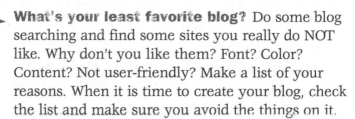

What's your least favorite blog? Do some blog searching and find some sites you really do NOT like. Why don't you like them? Font? Color? Content? Not user-friendly? Make a list of your reasons. When it is time to create your blog, check the list and make sure you avoid the things on it.

BRAIN JAM:
IITYWTMWYLMA?
(If I tell you what this means, will you leave me alone?)

Interested in some of the more unusual blogger abbreviations seen in the blogosphere lately? Here are a few:

FOAFOAGF — Father of a friend of a girlfriend

ILY — I love you

TGAL — Think Globally, Act Locally

UTT — Under the Table

YMMV — Your Mileage May Vary

Ready, set, go! List all the abbreviations you can think of that you use in e-mail and instant messages. Write out the full meaning of each one. How many did you come up with? Are any of them appropriate for your school project?

weblog

Internet

personal blog

conversation

Internet

To

politic

weblog

online journ

32

FRANKLIN
CHAPTER 2
WATTS

BUILD IT AND THEY WILL COME

How to Create a Weblog

F.W.'S
SPIDER
WEBLOG

How to Create a Weblog

Now that you have examined several blogs and thought about your own blog voice, it's time to get down to the business of creating a weblog. This chapter will help you plan out your assignment, organize your ideas, find a blog hosting service, and build that blog.

Planning, Purpose, and Prose

After you receive the assignment, your next step is to plan your strategy of attack by **identifying all the tasks you need to accomplish**. First, look over the assignment. Read it several times. Then, on a blank sheet of paper, list the components of the assignment. Generally speaking, your assignment will require you to:

- **Create a name or title for your weblog.**

- **Decide on a theme or topic.**

- **Write an initial posting.**

- **Request or call for posts in which readers provide additional information and insights on your topic.**

Look over the list you made and compare it to what the teacher gave you. **Did you miss any steps?** If so, put them on your list. **Are any of the steps confusing to you?** Don't wait! Go and talk to your teacher right away and get the clarification you need. You don't want to spend precious time trying to figure out the assignment or risk doing it wrong.

On the next few pages, you will see a sample of an assignment for an English class and an attack plan for that assignment. It is geared for students who have read **Homer's *Odyssey***. You need to create a weblog that discusses whether or not you believe that Odysseus was a hero. The sample assignment is followed by a sample attack plan template. It will show you all of the elements needed to complete the assignment, but it will be blank. The following page will show you the template again, filled in with the information you gathered to complete your task.

RESOURCES

Here are some great Web sites to check out for lots of tips, tricks, and ideas for starting your own blog:

http://www.createblog.com
http://blogjet.com/create_blog.php
http://www.blogger.com/start

SAMPLE ASSIGNMENT

In our reading of **Homer's *Odyssey***, the protagonist Odysseus exhibits the qualities of a hero, as well as a character with definite flaws. Create a weblog explaining whether or not you believe Odysseus was a hero. Your weblog must include:

- A title

- An introductory posting about whether or not you think Odysseus is a hero

- Two quotes supporting your point of view, plus a minimum of two paragraphs explaining in detail how these quotes support your opinion

- A call to other bloggers to state whether they agree or disagree with you. Encourage them to support their opinions with additional quotes from the text

- Three additional postings in response to bloggers' answers

- A concluding paragraph

You will be graded on completion of all elements in this assignment and the quality of your work. You will not be graded on the other bloggers' responses. Three classmates will be assigned to your blog to thoughtfully answer the question. They will be graded separately for their postings.

WEBLOG ASSIGNMENT

The assignment weblog must include:

1. **A title**
   Ideas for my title include:

2. **An introductory posting that states whether or not I believe Odysseus was a hero**
   I believe that Odysseus was:

3. **Two quotes supporting my stance**
   Quote 1:
   Quote 2:

4. **The reasons the quotes I've chosen support my stance**
   They are supportive because:

5. **The explanation of the quotes must be at least two paragraphs long.**
   Is it? _____Yes _____No—I need to get more information on this.

6. **I need to connect with the other three bloggers assigned to post a response. I should remind them to support their opinions with quotes from the text.**
   Their names are:

7. **Responses to each person's posting**
   First response posting date:

   Second response posting date:

   Third response posting date:

8. **A concluding paragraph**
   Ideas for this include:

37

WEBLOG ASSIGNMENT

SAMPLE ATTACK PLAN TEMPLATE FOR

COMPLETED

The assignment weblog must include:

1. A title
Ideas for my title include:

> Homeric Hero
>
> Odysseus's Dilemma

2. An introductory posting that states whether or not I believe Odysseus was a hero

> I believe that Odysseus was a hero but still flawed. He was clever and brave, yet sometimes a bit too full of himself.

3. Two quotes supporting my stance

> "I am Odysseus, son of Laertes, known before all men for the study of crafty designs, and my fame goes up to the heavens." (book 9, lines 19-20)

> "So the great soldier took his bow and bent it for the bowstring effortlessly. He drilled the axeheads clean, sprang and decanted arrows on the door sill, glared and drew again. This time he killed Antinoos." (book 24, lines 196-201)

SAMPLE ATTACK PLAN TEMPLATE FOR

4. The reasons the quotes I've chosen support my stance

> They are supportive because: The first quote shows the character's lack of humility as he brags of his abilities. He proclaims that his fame will reach all men, as well as up into heaven.

> On the other hand, the second quote points him out as strong, determined, and confident. These are all qualities of a hero.

5. The explanation of the quotes must be at least two paragraphs long.
Is it? __X__Yes ____No

6. I need to connect with the other three bloggers assigned to post a response. I should remind them to support their opinions with quotes from the text. Their names are:

> Sue Brown, Carol Chen, Mike Rosen

7. Responses to each person's posting
First response posting date: 12/01/06
Second response posting date: 12/04/06
Third response posting date: 12/05/06

8. A concluding paragraph

> Ideas for this include: a look at how most readers saw the character— as a hero, not as a hero, or as a combination of both. Any similarity in the quotes they chose? How did their opinions differ from mine?

Titles and Introductions

Let's look at the components of an Odysseus weblog assignment. The most important components are the **title** and the **introductory posting**. Why? Because **these items will entice readers to post**. (Sure, for your class assignment they may be required to post, but that doesn't mean you can't help them WANT to post something!)

Let's look at possible titles for our weblog:

ORDINARY	EXTRAORDINARY
Greek Guy	Odysseus: Hero or Zero?

The ordinary title doesn't explain the premise of the blog. The extraordinary title lets readers know that they should respond to whether or not they believe Odysseus is truly a hero or just a selfish man.

Now let's look at some possible introductory postings:

ORDINARY

Odysseus lost all his men on his way home. Lots of stuff happened to him. I think he was a hero.

EXTRAORDINARY

In Homer's *Odyssey*, Odysseus is cursed and thwarted by the gods on his journey home after the Trojan War. For twenty years, he endures many hardships by keeping one thing in mind: getting back to his wife, Penelope. Or is he really that interested in Penelope? Is he a hero who loves his family and his men? Or is he a selfish ruler who miserably fails his wife and his men? There are many examples in the story that can support both sides of the argument.

What do you believe? Let me know if you think Odysseus is a true hero or a big zero. Cite examples from the text that show me the strength of your argument. I believe that Odysseus was a hero, but flawed. Let's compare my opinion and supporting evidence to yours. Maybe together we can determine if this Greek figure really should be considered a hero.

The ordinary posting does little, if anything, to lead bloggers into responding. The extraordinary posting not only gives background, but also asks questions and explains to bloggers what is expected.

Reinforcements

To plan your weblog, you need to look carefully at the assignment and get organized. Be sure you know exactly what your teacher expects and then follow through by keeping track of the date of each posting. In the sample, the student needed to spend time looking for applicable evidence and determining what attributes constituted heroism. Although the assignment was for an English class, the same planning goes into any assignment, across the curriculum, and the creation of ANY blog—even a personal blog. You might wind up enjoying the assignment so much that you decide to join the blogosphere with your own personal weblog.

Even when you write a personal blog, you don't want to bore your readers. Let's look at two versions of a personal blog posting about the blogger's day at school.

ORDINARY

September 7, 2006

Today was the best day of my life. Everything I wanted to happen actually happened. I'm so lucky. Steve R. asked me to go to homecoming, and I got an A on the algebra test.

42

EXTRAORDINARY

September 7, 2006

Today was the best day of my life—ever. First, Steve R., who I've had a total and complete crush on, asked me to the homecoming dance. But he didn't just ask me in any ordinary way. Steve had all the guys in our fourth period class dress up like Scotsmen from Braveheart, *play drums, and then in a total Scot voice, just like Mel Gibson's in the movie, asked me to homecoming. Our school's theme this year is "A Wonderful World," and the sophomore class has chosen Scotland as our float country. So it was pretty cool that he kept in theme and got all those other guys to play along to ask me. I'm excited!*

Just to add icing to an already perfect day, I aced my math test. Anyone who has Mr. McClargonomic knows how difficult his tests are—especially because he's the worst teacher on the planet. I literally have to teach myself how to do the problems from the textbook every night. Whatever! I'm going to the dance with Steve, and he made me feel like a princess in class.

The ordinary blog doesn't provide any examples or interesting stories. Who wants to read one-liners that don't tell you anything? After all, why do you think so many people tune in to reality television? A personal blog is the reality television of the Internet. **The extraordinary blog showcases specific examples** and tells the story of how the blogger's day went. You can feel the excitement and see the guys all dressed in *Braveheart* costumes.

So Here's the Scoop

Using precise language will help you create extraordinary blog postings. Here are a few examples.

VAGUE WORD:	PRECISE WORDS:
stuff	events, happenings, belongings, collection, bits and pieces, gear, equipment
good	fantastic, great, unbelievable, wonderful, incredible, excellent, delightful, skillful, high-quality, first class
bad	awful, terrible, dreadful, appalling, ghastly, dire, wicked, cruel, evil, horrible, catastrophic, alarming
hard	challenging, difficult, taxing, demanding, arduous, grueling, problematic, tricky, frustrating
fun	enjoyable, amusing, entertaining, pleasurable, exciting

Even if your own weblog focuses on nothing but sneakers, you'll still need:

- a title,

- an introductory posting,

- a call to others asking for their comments about your fascination with athletic footwear.

The organization needed for the class assignment remains the same for the personal blog about sneakers. So whatever your blog may be about, plan your attack well.

Where's the Party? Host Services

Now we've arrived at the technical end of creating weblogs. Writing is probably second nature by now. Since kindergarten, you've been learning how to put pen to paper. But programming? That's not really second nature for most people. In fact, some of us can barely figure out how to accomplish what we need to on our computers. You may be one of those technologically adept people who want to learn programming and build their own weblogs and Web sites, but that's a completely different book!

For the purpose of our assignments, we'll look at blog hosting services. These services:

- are inexpensive (sometimes free!),

- lead you step-by-step through the process of creating a site.

Basically, you sign up and then fill in the blanks—like you did when you created an e-mail account. With technological advances, it's never been easier to create your own online world.

Going Blog Host Shopping

You need to consider several things when shopping for a hosting service. First, of course, is talking to your parents about it. They will probably want to know what you are doing before you make any commitments— especially one that may require a fee. Explain your assignment or describe the personal blog you'd like to create. If they aren't familiar with blogs, it is probably a good idea to show them some online samples.

As you shop, **find out if the host charges a fee or is free.** Many are free, but that often means that there will be more advertising on the site. For your assignments, a free service should be fine. But if you choose to go the extra mile and want your own domain name (instead of the one chosen for you by the hosting service), a site free from annoying pop-ups, and more design elements to choose from, you will want to check out premium services. They can run anywhere from five to thirty dollars a month.

According to Rebecca Blood, author of ***The Weblog Handbook: Practical Advice on Creating and Maintaining Your Blog*** (Perseus Publishing, 2002), free services often come with some significant drawbacks. Service may be slow and there may be outages, or times when you just can't access the server, during which you will be unable to read or update your Web site. "These services go through cycles as they become popular," she writes, "their equipment becomes overloaded, they upgrade their machines, and then eventually become overloaded again." Despite this, most services do try their best to provide good service to their users.

Blood recommends that you ask yourself a few important questions about the server and site before making a decision:

- Can you easily identify how to create and delete an entry?

- Can you easily change the way your site looks?

- How do you add the name of your weblog to the page?

- Does this service offer clear instructions?

- Is it easy to find help when you need it?

- Do you need to read the directions before you can actually use the service or are many of the available functions easily understandable just by looking?

- Are there user forums where you can ask questions?

Her final piece of advice is to carefully evaluate the products and choose the service that you find easiest to use.

The space you receive on a free hosting service— about twenty megabytes or more—will be sufficient for your assignments. Should you become a gung-ho blogger and need more space, check into those premium services or purchase your own blogging software that you can customize to your server. Here are a few hosting services for you to check out:

http://www.blogger.com

http://www.diaryland.com

http://www.livejournal.com

http://www.weblogger.com

http://www.xanga.com

The Master of My Domain

If you want your own domain name, here is the basic procedure to follow:

- **Choose a domain name**—a process that takes some thought. It can be hard to find one that isn't already taken. Try typing in the one you want and see if it's available. If it isn't, many sites will offer you alternative suggestions to try.

- **Register the name you chose with a registration service.** Network Solutions is popular and one of the oldest, but there are many others out there. Follow the online instructions, including choosing the length of time you want to sign up for. Most services offer terms of from one to ten years; two years is the most common choice.

- **Choose a host.** Now you're off and running. Blog on!

RESOURCES

For additional information, check out "Blogging 101: Hosting Your Own Blog" at:

http://www.webraw.com/quixtar/archives/2005/04/blogging_101_hosting_your_own_blog.php

Log, Blog, Post, Edit

Once you choose your plan and register, you will access your account and begin building your blog, following the step-by-step questions and templates on the hosting service. Have your writing ready. The host service will lead you through the process of:

- **logging on to your blog;**

- **choosing design elements;**

- **using customization tools;**

- **posting, editing posts;**

- **managing your blog.**

When you create a blog, you get to make all of the decisions about who can post to your blog. There are three basic options:

1 An open blog automatically posts anyone's comments to your blog.

2 A moderated blog allows you to review bloggers' posts before they hit, so you can delete those you do not want added to your page.

3 A closed blog does not allow any posts at all—you are the sole writer.

For the assignments described in this book, you will be using moderated and closed sites. Some will require classmates to post to your blog while others will require your entries only.

When you are ready to begin writing postings, chances are good that you will run into Mr. Blog Writer's Block somewhere along the way. You are supposed to post and you cannot think of a thing to say. Here are a few suggestions to get rid of Mr. Block. They come from Sheila Ann Manuel Coggins in About.com's guide to Weblogs:

1 Check your email and see if something inspires you.

2 Go blog hopping—go to your favorites or to brand new ones. What is everyone talking about?

3 Turn on the news. What is the latest headline?

4 Create a list. Top ten. Favorites. Things to avoid at all costs. Current wishes.

5 Look through a photo album, yearbook, magazine, or scrapbook for an idea.

6 Pinpoint a question you have always had and then research it. Put your findings on your blog.

7 Walk away. Take a shower. Get the mail. Do your homework. Come back later and see if you have an idea.

"But just who reads blogs? It's not in the nature of the medium to commission demographic surveys, but I've noticed that lawyers, scientists and (naturally) media types seem particularly common visitors. Los Angeles blogger Matt Welch describes as his most avid readers 'a gay conservative bed & breakfast owner; a retired Republican cop in Pomona; a Naderite expatriate in New Zealand; a liberal literature professor fed up with campus radicalism; a music freak from Minnesota; a thoughtful and pessimistic lefty housewife in Nebraska; a pissed-off quadrilingual Czech-born grad student in Berkeley; a top editor at a major science-fiction publishing house . . . these people are supposed to have nothing in common, according to the old politics.'"

—Catherine Seipp, writer,
American Journalism Review

PROJECT JUMP START

Find three hosting services and list three reasons why you would or wouldn't use each one. Think of it like shopping for a car. What are you looking for in style, color, and safety features? Carefully weigh the pros and cons of each alternative. Your hosting service is the vehicle that will get you around the Web, so be picky and make a thoughtful decision before you insert the key!

BRAIN JAM:
TECHNICAL ASSISTANCE

Are you intimidated by the technical aspects of creating a blog? The best way to hone your skills is to try out the software and play around with it. An easy place to practice is MySpace.com. It's simple to create a personal profile and begin blogging on this site. Many teenagers blog and post on MySpace.com because the technical instructions are so easy to follow. You can also have some fun checking out other kids' blogs as you work on your own!

layout

copyright

target audience

conversation

editor

Ez

publis

1

publisher

reporter

STYLE AND FORM

The Electronic Magazine

The Electronic Magazine

You see magazines on newsstands everywhere. Many of those same magazines have online versions called ezines. Just like the *e* in *e-mail*, the *e* in *ezine* stands for electronic. Electronic magazines—ezines—are just like the magazines you buy at the newsstand, except you read them online. Electronic magazines usually contain content not seen in the newsstand version, and vice versa. Some ezines charge for a subscription (often delivered to your e-mail inbox); some do not.

Ezines quickly took hold in the electronic world as soon as aspiring publishers learned how inexpensively they could produce a magazine if thcy didn't have to:

- **print copies,**
- **mail copies,**
- **find distribution channels.**

Internet search engines made it easier to market the publications. Meanwhile, regional and national magazines launched their online equivalents. From fashion to sports, from science to shoes, from books to bands—magazines cover a myriad of subjects. The power of publishing is formidable.

So let's learn the basics of ezine publishing. Put on your reporter's hat. It's time to create an ezine.

The 4-1-1—A Web Site Versus an Ezine

You may be wondering, "What's the difference between a Web site and an ezine?" There is one main difference: flowing content. Web sites are static in nature, meaning their content rarely, if ever, changes. A city Web site, for example, covers all the services that a city offers its citizens. Those services typically don't change. The fire, police, water, and other departments all operate and function the same way day after day. The city Web site is static—it doesn't "move."

An ezine, however, covers new stories, updates sections, and showcases original content on a daily, weekly, monthly, or quarterly basis. Fluid content drives the publication. Just as you pick up your favorite magazine each month to read fresh stories and get the latest information on a subject, people read ezines for their current content. You wouldn't buy a magazine that had the same stories in it month after month after month, right? Would you go back to the same Web site every month and read it if the content NEVER changed?

For EXample

Let's say you're into motorcycles, and you hit a site with an article about an innovative Ducati (a specific brand of racing motorbikes). You like the story, and the site is packed with great information about racing, so you return to it the next week to see if there's anything new. Nothing. You go back again in two weeks, but still no change. Pretty soon, if the only article ever displayed is the Ducati piece, you won't be going back. Ezines update information. Ezines are magazines, plain and simple. As such, they change.

RESOURCE

To get familiar with ezines, you need to see some. Check out this Web site for links to family and teen oriented ezines:

http://www.goezines.com/Home_and_Family/Family/Kids _and_Teens/index.html

Ready, Aim, Fire—Hitting Your Target Audience

The people who read a magazine make up that publication's audience. You, as publisher of your own electronic magazine, will also cater to your readers. All publishers and editors of a magazine take into consideration the demographics (age, location, income, and interests) of their readers in order to better provide the group with stories that interest them. Everything from the title of the magazine to the layout to the content has the reader in mind.

A women's magazine for college-educated females between the ages of twenty-one and thirty-five will probably explore careers, fashion, fitness, and many other topics that typically interest this group. You probably won't find a story on big game hunting with the guys between its covers. But then again, if market research shows that your female readers share in the desire for action sports and high-risk adventure, you just might find that story. **The key to any publication's longevity is finding its niche audience and writing for that group.**

❤ **Cat lovers read cat magazines.**

❤ **Dog lovers read dog magazines.**

❤ **Fashion lovers read fashion magazines.**

Your task will be to determine your audience and write for it. Your teacher, of course, will be a reader but may require you to write as if you were in a different period of time for a particular group of people.

So Here's the Scoop

When looking for your favorite magazine online, like **Car and Driver** or **Seventeen**, don't assume that the ezine address will be www.nameofpublicationinserted.com. Sometimes, multiple magazines are listed and linked together on one Web site. For example, *http://www.ivillage.com* is an ezine that, along with original content, showcases several other magazines, such as **Allure** and **Redbook**, on its site. The best way to find the online equivalent of your preferred newsstand magazine is by Googling the magazine's name in quotes and then putting the word *magazine* after your quoted title.

TIP FILE

Demographics are the characteristics of a population. The demographics of a magazine, therefore, are the characteristics of the typical readers.

The **editor** of a magazine is the person who assigns the stories to writers, manages the production of the magazine, often writes pieces for the publication, and sometimes copyedits the content. Think about it: you will be the editor of your ezine. In fact, you will be the editor in chief!

PROJECT JUMP START

Gather up five magazines. Look at the covers and write down who you think the typical reader of the publication is. Try to guess the typical reader's:

- **Gender**
- **Age**
- **Lifestyle**
- **Home life**
- **Potential hobbies**

Sneak a peek at the table of contents, the advertisements, and the design of the magazine to help guide you.

Now, explain why you gave the answers you did. What did you see that led to your profile of the typical reader?

Exchange magazines with a classmate. Now do the same exercise with your classmate's magazine. When you are finished with the exercise, discuss your findings with each other. You'll most likely find you both determined the same demographics.

BRAIN JAM:
Getting Past Writer's Block

When your mind goes blank and your fingers are just sitting on the keys and not moving, give one of these ideas a try:

- Pick a number (ten is always popular) and say 10 TIPS for . . . . you fill in the blank. Make it relate to your ezine's main focus.

- Tell the readers how to do something. Give them directions or instructions on how to make or create a project related to your ezine's topic.

- Write a review of a book, movie, product, or anything else you can review with knowledge and still relate to your ezine's purpose.

- Bring in current events and show how they relate to your ezine topic. Write an editorial on the subject.

64

CHAPTER 4

GO EZINE, ACTIVATE

How to Publish an Ezine

How to Publish an Ezine

Now that you know what an ezine is, it's time to find out how to put one together. Just like blogs, there are free Web site hosting services that provide templates that will walk you through building your Web site. Your ezine is technically a Web site, after all. You'll just be changing a few stories now and then.

Topic and Copy

Magazines contain stories that are planned out by the editors in advance. The stories all relate to the theme of the magazine. The online version of *Time* magazine prints content from its newsstand edition as well as original content written solely for the Internet edition. Those features relate to news and culture. The theme of the magazine drives the content. The copy is also varied. While one feature will be an in-depth article of three thousand words, other pieces might only be two hundred words and give quick information on the topic at hand. For your assignment, you'll need to write stories related to the topic your teacher assigns.

You Look Marvelous!— Making Your Ezine Visually Appealing

Think about a magazine that you like to read. Imagine flipping through it. What do you look for? What different elements go into making it look appealing to you? Most likely, they break down into five components:

- **content**
- **font and spacing**
- **colors**
- **photographs**
- **layout**

Let's take a look at each one of these factors.

Content is the most important component of any magazine. The *New Yorker* is a prime example of a content-heavy magazine that flies off the shelves. People do not read the *New Yorker* for the ads or the design. The *New Yorker* sells because of its fascinating news stories and fiction writing. Does that mean the magazine—and its online version—aren't visually appealing? Of course not. Designers choose distinctive fonts and an appealing layout.

RESOURCE

To take a look at the online version of *New Yorke*r magazine, go to *http://www.newyorker.com/*

TIP FILE

Those savvy about the World Wide Web know that you can access and download free programs called open source programs for your personal use. These programs provide software for many different uses that you can share and even modify. In this text, you'll find several sites that provide open source programs for both Web sites and weblogs. Many programs are also available for purchase. These offer more bells and whistles, but many of the free programs still offer enough to get you off the ground and writing!

Font and Spacing

Choose your font and stay consistent. Don't go overboard and use a different font on every story or every page. It'll look messy, and you'll appear indecisive. You'll seem like an amateur if you try to throw every font up on the screen. My advice? Pick one font that "feels" like the ezine you are creating. If, for example you are creating an ezine for an American history class, choose a font like **Bookman Old Style.** The font indicates a bygone era and will add visual effect to your words.

If you are going for a newspaper look, you may want **Arial** for your headlines and **Times New Roman** for copy.

For a casual, friendly, laid back look to your text, why not use **Comic Sans MS**?

For straightforward, clean copy, choose from Garamond, **Franklin Gothic Book**, or Georgia.

Avoid using the more off the wall fonts like Curlz, *Lucida Handwriting,* or Kashmir because they may look fascinating but they are just too hard to read.

A note about **font size**: never go smaller than ten picas, or points. It is too small to read comfortably, especially on a computer screen. On the flip side, don't make it too large—eighteen picas or bigger—either. Twelve to sixteen picas is typical. Give some thought to **line spacing** as well. Single-spaced sentences, if you have dense copy, are going to be difficult to read. Experiment with one and a half or two spaces between the lines to determine what looks best to your eyes.

5 point type   10 point type   15 point type

Colors

Choose colors. Most of the templates that you will use to create your Web page will offer an array of colors from which to choose your background, banner, and other colors. Use some common sense when you pick them. Your favorite colors may be purple and orange, but they may not be your best choice. Be sure to take the time to look at your ezine from the reader's point of view and not just from your own. You don't want to have a dark text color and a dark background because the two elements will blur together. **Play around with two colors, perhaps three, that complement each other and—like your font—suggest the theme of your work.**

TIP FILE

Warning!

Never publish your phone number or address on any ezine or weblog. Doing so could make you vulnerable to stalkers, predators, and other criminals. Publishing a blog or an ezine should be fun and safe. Reduce your chances of encountering problems by taking precautions.

If your ezine assignment covers the 1960s, choose bright colors that were in fashion during those days. But if your ezine assignment details botany and plant life, you might choose greens and browns to showcase the prominent colors of your topic. **Colors should reinforce your ideas and not distract from the content.** Imagine if you splattered red, green, black, purple, gray, and orange on a page about photosynthesis. You'd distract the reader from your story with all the colors.

Graphics

Let's talk about graphics. Have you ever read a magazine without pictures or art? I didn't think so. In fact, more likely you've gone through magazines that are virtually ALL pictures or art. Ezines need to incorporate graphics also, in order to maintain interest. You will want to include photographs, cartoons, drawings, and clip art.

To put your own photos into your ezine, you need a scanner or a digital camera. Since these pictures belong to you, you don't have to worry about obtaining permission to use them (except from your parents and the people in the pictures). Be sure to write a caption for each photo—you may know who the people are and where they are, but your readers probably don't. The caption should help tie the picture to the text, but try not to reuse a statement from the text as the caption. Make it additional information that supports the topic of your article or story.

If you want to use pictures from another site, you must get permission first or you may be breaking important copyright laws. The same goes for logos, drawings, and other illustrations. If they didn't come from you, you must have written permission to use them.

The exception to this is the **free clip art found on the Web**. These are images you can sprinkle throughout your ezine to give it character and sparkle, and no permission is required. While there are many choices found on the net, here are a few to get you started:

http://www.allfree-clipart.com/

http://www.1clipart.com/

http://classroomclipart.com/

For your ezine, **it is best to use action photos if you can.** In an astronomy class, for example, your ezine could have a picture of Neil Armstrong walking on the moon. How about a personal ezine on fashion? Don't use a picture of a shirt on a rack. Instead, find a model wearing the shirt while doing some activity. **Whether you use color or black-and-white photography depends on the assignment.** Use black-and-white photography if the mood or tone of your assignment suggests it. Use color photography for a contemporary topic.

Layout

The layout and design of your ezine is how you put all of the above factors together. Placement of photos is an important part of the overall look and balance of your pages. Generally speaking, choose one central photo for each page and perhaps two smaller ones to illustrate other stories.

The most important story within your ezine should appear as the headline with the most prominent photo. No more than two other stories should appear on the opening page and the corresponding photographs shouldn't overpower the stories. You don't want to distract your reader with too much on one page. **Your goal is to eliminate visual clutter.** Beyond the main page of stories, you can use a pull down menu and other template options for additional pages and articles.

TIP FILE
Warning!

You are, of course, going to want to copy photos and other information from the Internet to post to your blog or ezine, but beware—copyright restrictions may apply. Always get the permission of the original owner before cutting and pasting anything to your pages. Clip art and free art pages do abound online, so use those services when you can.

Did I Write That?

One thing you will definitely want to steer clear of in your blogs and ezines is libel. **You have a right to free speech, but you don't have the right to harm someone with your words.** And if you do, you can be sued and jailed for libel. So just what is libel? Here is a quick reference to help you understand libel, so you can make sure that your work—for class or pleasure—won't get you into trouble.

Libel is any FALSE statement, written or broadcast, that brings any other person into PUBLIC hatred, contempt, or ridicule; and/or causes that person to be shunned or avoided; and/or injures a person in his or her business, profession, or career.

But if you've read about libel cases, you'll know there have been times when the person bringing the legal action (or, the plaintiff) has not proven the statement made was false, yet still won the case. Why is that? Because the court decided that the writer intended to cause the person harm (or malice), so what was printed was indeed libelous.

So how do you keep something like that from happening to you? **Simply tell the unbiased, nonmalicious truth.**

- Don't write anything meant to harm someone

- Make sure your facts are correct

And because this book is not about legal issues and can't provide you with legal counsel, in the event that something happens, you need to contact an attorney. Schools usually provide legal counsel to their newspaper and yearbook classes. You or your teacher will want to find out where to go in the event of a libel allegation. Contact the newspaper adviser on your campus or the principal of your school.

Heads Up!

Free Speech

The First Amendment to the U.S. Constitution states: "Congress shall make no law respecting an establishment of religion, or prohibiting the free exercise thereof; or abridging the freedom of speech, or of the press; or the right of the people peaceably to assemble, and to petition the government for a redress of grievances."

When it comes to weblogs and ezines, freedom of speech and freedom of the press are important rights. The U.S. Constitution guarantees your right to post messages on a blog or create an Internet magazine that states your own perspectives and editorials. When you enter the realm of a school assignment, however, your rights may be altered by your school's rules and regulations. When you are in school, working on a class assignment, or involved in a school-sponsored activity, you must follow the guidelines given to you by your instructor or adviser.

EXPRESS YOURSELF

The American Booksellers Foundation for Free Expression Web site—**http://www.abffe.org**—is a great resource for anyone writing an ezine or blog. It contains lots of information on your right of free expression. And you never know how your writing will evolve. Maybe you'll turn your blog into a book someday!

PROJECT JUMP START

⭐ Take a look at two
or three ezines and answer
the following questions:

- Are more than two fonts used?

- Is the font size readable?

- Do the pages look cluttered?

- Is photography and artwork incorporated in the ezine?

- How many images are used on each page?

- Do the photos used show action?

BRAIN JAM:
Bring on the Guests!

Liven up your ezine with an interview of someone who has experience or education related to the topic of your ezine. You can conduct a phone, e-mail, or face-to-face interview in a question-and-answer format and post it on your ezine (with the interviewee's permission, of course) for others to read and learn from.

If you want to take this step just a little further, have your guest write an essay, commentary, or editorial for your ezine and post it there. After all, readers are interested in what people other than you have to say on the topic.

title

linking

blogosphere

quotes

Internet

bl

quotes

t

linking

online journ

FRANKLIN CHAPTER 5 WATTS

READY, SET, BLOG!

Projects to Get You Rave Reviews from Your Teachers

Projects to Get You Rave Reviews from Your Teachers

Now it's time to show your extraordinary abilities. Here are some assignments that run across disciplines— meaning that **these assignments can be used in most of the subjects you study in school, such as history, art, and science.** In most cases, just by writing a blog or an ezine, you will be meeting your state's educational standards for language arts. Nevertheless, some English assignments are also included.

Now it's your turn to become a weblog host and call all bloggers (your classmates) together to create extraordinary blogs.

Language Arts

Any blog that you create will most likely demonstrate and strengthen your language arts skills.

Creating a blog can:

- help you improve your punctuation, capitalization, and grammar;

- teach you lessons about sentence variety and vocabulary use;

- give you practice in organizing your thoughts and writing out logical statements and responses.

As a bonus, you may have so much fun creating the blog that you forget you are actually doing something educational!

Here are a few ideas for blogs that are especially appropriate for teaching language arts skills.

ASSIGNMENT 1

SHOW OFF!

Create a weblog all about your likes and dislikes—nothing rude, please. You may use any of the free weblog software available online but you must ensure that the students in your class and the instructor can post on the blog. Your blog must include:

1. **A title**—How would you describe your blog?

2. **An introductory paragraph**—What does your blog cover, and what is its purpose?

3. **Your entries**—Include at least one paragraph, posted each week, covering a topic of interest or concern to you that asks other bloggers what they think.

4. **An evaluation of the responses you received**—You will critically examine the postings you received on your blog in a paragraph, using quotes from the blogs to support your assertions.

5. **Posting due dates:**

    1st _____

    2nd _____

    3rd _____

    4th _____

What's in a Name?

Let's talk about titles for a moment. They are very important. A good title gets people's attention and makes them curious to know more. Would you want to see a movie called *A Good Guy Makes the Wrong Decision* or would you rather see *Revenge of the Sith*? Would you read a book called *Four Friends and a Pair of Jeans* or would you be more intrigued by *Sisterhood of the Traveling Pants*? The title for your blog is just as important. Whether it is for fun or for a class assignment, you need a **relevant** and **attention-grabbing** title.

In this first assignment, the blog is all about you! Think about a great title for it—but don't just use your name.

ORDINARY	EXTRAORDINARY
Lynne's Blog	Dara's Stars and Celestial Heavens

Here I've used myself as an example to show the difference between the ordinary and the extraordinary. Let's say I'm starting a blog that will cover my love of the stars and astronomy. If I just titled it "Lynne's Blog," I'd have buried a good topic in my ordinary name. And did I mention that the name Lynne has nothing to do with astronomy? But if I took on a pseudonym such as Dara (meaning "star" in Cambodian) and titled the Web page "Dara's Stars and Celestial Heavens," I'd have hit on something extraordinary.

You want the title of your blog to be something people will remember. A friend of mine hosts a weblog for career women to chat after work. Instead of calling it "Career Women," she gave her site the title "Black Dresses and Pearls," to connote the sophistication of the women blogging.

ORDINARY	EXTRAORDINARY
Career Women	Black Dresses and Pearls

Now it's your turn. Let's look at some ordinary titles and see what extraordinary titles you can come up with to replace them. Remember—you want to grab a person's attention, not make them yawn and pass right on by.

ORDINARY TITLES

Jim's Photographs	Moments in Basketball
8th Grade	
Finding a Job	Stephen King's Books

ASSIGNMENT 2

In **Harper Lee's** novel *To Kill a Mockingbird*, the author used the mockingbird as a symbol of innocence and its fragility. Many authors use symbols in their work. A symbol is a person, place, thing, or event that has meaning in itself and also stands for something more than itself. For instance, an olive branch is often a symbol for peace, as is a dove. A skull and crossbones means death; a cross is a symbol of Christianity.

Recognizing symbols in literature is an important skill. Your task is to create a weblog that looks at literary symbols. You may want to discuss, for example, Harper Lee's use of the mockingbird as a symbol—what the bird represents and how the image is used with different characters (Tom Robinson, Boo Radley, Scout) within the novel. You need to include:

1. **A title**—remember to make it interesting. "Innocence Shattered" is much more attention getting than something like "Lee's Mockingbird."

2. **An introduction** that includes the reference to Lee's mockingbird and requests that bloggers discuss the symbolism often associated with songbirds.

3. **Three more entries**, drawing upon any of the literature you've read. Quote the entry (the lines from the book), provide the source (title of the book or short story) and then explain in a paragraph what you believe is symbolic in the passage. Here are some examples:

- The blood on Macbeth's wife's hands in **Shakespeare's** play *Macbeth*

- The porridge in **Charles Dickens's** novel *Oliver Twist*

- The sword in the books about **King Arthur** and **Camelot**

4. **Open the blog up for discussion** among your classmates and ask them to find other sources of symbolism in the books they have read, the music they listen to, or the world around them.

5. **Post responses to your classmates' comments** and relate them to how Lee uses the symbol of the mockingbird.

TIP FILE

When you discuss symbols in your weblog, be sure to really explain all the possible meanings and nuances of the symbol. It'll make the difference between an ordinary blog and an extraordinary one.

Don't forget that your blog is more interesting if it includes some graphics.

ORDINARY

Mockingbirds are generally considered to be harmless. They are nice birds that do not bother farmers or homeowners.

EXTRAORDINARY

MOCKINGBIRDS ARE GENERALLY CONSIDERED TO BE HARMLESS.

AS ATTICUS FINCH SAYS IN THE STORY, "MOCKINGBIRDS DON'T DO ANYTHING BUT MAKE MUSIC FOR US TO ENJOY. THEY DON'T EAT PEOPLE'S GARDENS, DON'T NEST IN THE CORNCRIBS, THEY DON'T DO ONE THING BUT JUST SING THEIR HEARTS OUT FOR US."

Notice that a quote from the book is added to the text. **And the use of images makes the text more visually appealing.** After all, don't you prefer books with pictures?

ASSIGNMENT 3

You'll be blogging solo for this assignment. This blog will be a chapter-by-chapter showcase of a novel you read in class. Your blog will include:

1. **A title**—not the title of the book!

2. **An introductory paragraph** announcing what you will be covering in the blog

3. **Chapter observations**—For each chapter, choose a few lines or a paragraph that particularly grabs you or makes you think. List the page number and the text you will be exploring. From there, detail in a paragraph why you chose that text. What about it did you find interesting?

4. **Chapter devices**—For each chapter, find one of the following literary elements and discuss its relevance to the overall novel:

   - **Foreshadowing:** subtle suggestions within the story that give the reader hints about something that may happen later on

   - **Metaphor or Simile:** a comparison between two unlike things (if it uses "like" or "as," it is a simile)

   - **Theme:** the main meaning or idea within the book

   - **Symbolism:** where one person, place or thing represents more than itself within a story

   Remember that you must create two entries for each chapter: one on a section from the chapter that you found interesting and why you found it interesting and another that discusses a literary element within that section.

5. **Finally,** upon completion of the chapter entries, you will **post an entry that discusses your overall perception of the book.**

Picture This

Want to make your solo blog extraordinary? Try linking pictures that you find online for the characters in the novels that you write about. Let's say you are blogging about all the scenes and acts in **Romeo and Juliet**. If you choose to discuss something outrageous that Romeo says, why not link to a picture of Romeo from one of the film versions? Or how about gaining some perspective on the geography associated with the play? Find "fair Verona" and link an image right into your blog or embed a link for others to follow. Although this may be your blog and no one else may post on it, you still want readers to find a variety of information when they visit.

ORDINARY

Verona is a city in northern Italy. Tradition says it is the setting for **Romeo and Juliet**. If you visit the city, you can see the tomb of Juliet, Romeo's house, and Juliet's house.

EXTRAORDINARY

Ah, fair Verona! This city, traditionally said to be the home of **Shakespeare's *Romeo and Juliet***, lies in northern Italy at the foot of the Lessini Mountains. The Adige River forms a half circle around it. Visitors to the city will be treated to many wonderful sights, including ancient Roman ruins and the homes of Romeo and Juliet. Just in case you have no plans to travel to Italy soon, here is a link that will give you a virtual tour of this fair city:

http://www.virtourist.com/europe/verona/

A statue of Juliet in the courtyard of the house in Verona where Shakespeare's Juliet is said to have lived.

ASSIGNMENT 4

THE JOURNALIST IN YOU

Your assignment is to find ten articles during the next two weeks that all relate to a single current event—a war, political unrest, social reform, weather disasters, anything that's been in the news. You will analyze and give your opinion about each of the articles. Then you will invite others to comment.

1. **First, choose a topic that interests you.**

2. **Choose a title.**

3. **Begin your blog by introducing the first in the series of articles you've gleaned. Be sure to give credit to the author by listing the publication it appeared in, its title, the author's name, and the date it was published.**

4. **Provide your readers with a synopsis of the article and then give your perspective on it. If the topic is controversial, support your opinion.**

5. **Give bloggers an invitation to login and comment on your articles.**

6. **Repeat steps 3 through 5 for each of the clips* you pull.**

* In the past, when you pulled an article from a publication, you clipped it out with scissors (pre-computer "cut and paste" days). When you hear or read a reference to clips, it means articles pulled for research or for an author to showcase his or her work in a portfolio. If you print your blog pages out, you have just created your first published clips!

ASSIGNMENT 4—COMPLETED

Your assignment is to find ten articles during the next two weeks that all relate to a current event—a war, political unrest, social reform, weather disasters, anything that's been in the news. You will analyze and give your opinion about each of the articles. Then you will invite others to comment.

1. First, choose a topic that interests you.

Intelligent Design versus Evolution

2. Choose a title.

God or Gorillas? The Ongoing Controversy about Human Origins

3. Begin your blog by introducing the first in the series of articles you've gleaned. Be sure to give credit to the author by listing the publication it appeared in, its title, the author's name, and the date it was published.

According to an article called, "Pennsylvania Intelligent Design Trial Ends" from the November 5, 2005 online version of *Science Daily*, a federal judge must now decide if teaching intelligent design (often used synonymously with "creationism") should be taught along with evolution in today's high school biology classes.

ASSIGNMENT 4—CONTINUED

THE JOURNALIST IN YOU

4. Provide your readers with a synopsis of the article and then give your perspective on it. If the topic is controversial, support your opinion.

SYNPOSIS

This article tells about the well-publicized trial that has been going on for weeks in Pennsylvania. A group of parents sued the public school system because its leaders wanted its teachers to teach intelligent design as a scientific theory of how the world began. This trial is based on the constitutional right to separation of church and state. It has been a very emotionally heated trial with experts and passionate witnesses on both sides of the issue.

THE JOURNALIST IN YOU

MY PERSPECTIVE

I feel that the parents are right in what they are asking for. They are demanding that the theory of intelligent design not be taught as science. They are simply requiring that it be taught as a religious philosophy rather than a scientific theory. I agree completely and hope that the judge does too!

5. **Give bloggers an invitation to login and comment on your articles.**

   Do you agree or disagree with my opinion? Why? Why not? Post your response to the article and my thoughts and let's talk!

6. **Repeat steps 3 through 5 for each of the clips you pull.**

History

History isn't just a thing of the past. The political, economic, and social actions of today were shaped by historical figures and their choices. Current events will shape our future.

Many prominent weblogs have a geopolitical slant. They discuss the relationships among:

- **politics,**
- **geography,**
- **demography,**
- **economics.**

Now it's your turn to show off your history savvy with these weblog assignments.

ASSIGNMENT 1

Two religious faiths that have had a profound effect on our world are Christianity and Islam. Create a weblog in which you call upon bloggers to discuss significant events in the history of these religions, from the beginnings of Christianity in the first century and Islam's founding in the seventh century. How did these events lead to Christian and Islamic dominance of Europe and the Middle East by the end of the medieval period?

Your weblog must include:

1. A title

2. A paragraph introducing bloggers to the purpose of the blog

3. A short essay (your first blog entry, two to three paragraphs long) giving your insight into the question at hand (i.e., What do you think the significant events were that led to Christian and Islamic dominance of Europe and the Middle East by the end of the medieval period?)

4. A summation of the viewpoints you received from bloggers as your final entry

Your blog will stay "live" for three weeks. Ask at least four classmates (bloggers) to write entries on your site. Promise them that you will return the favor!

May I Quote You?

When you include quotes from famous historical figures, you help history come alive in the pages of your blog. The quotes may even help you compare and contrast two historical figures.

ORDINARY

Jesus Christ was the founder of Christianity. His followers believe that he is the son of God who was sent to save them. Likewise, Muhammad is the founder of Islam. He is believed to be God's messenger on Earth.

EXTRAORDINARY

Jesus Christ and Muhammad are the founders of two of the world's great religions. Though Christians and Muslims have often clashed throughout history, the founders of their religions had many similar messages. Take these two quotes, for example:

"No man is a true believer unless he desireth for his brother that which he desireth for himself."
        —Muhammad

"You should love your neighbor as you love yourself."
        —Jesus Christ

ASSIGNMENT 2

The Renaissance period (the fourteenth through seventeenth centuries) created a transition between medieval and modern times. It is characterized by a flowering of classical literature, art, and the beginnings of modern science. In a weblog:

- Describe three to five significant events and discoveries that sparked the Renaissance.

- Discuss the cultural growth that resulted.

To do this, you must:

1. **Give your blog a title.**

2. **Write an introductory paragraph** describing the Renaissance period.

3. **Choose three to five events or discoveries of this era.** Write at least two paragraphs about each one in which you detail who was involved, when it happened, and what cultural growth came about as a result of the event or discovery.

4. **Invite others to respond to your choices** and add what they think were the most significant events and discoveries and why.

5. **Write a paragraph summarizing what you learned during the creation of your blog.**

To complete this assignment, all you need to do is describe major events and the cultural significance of the Renaissance period. But if that's all you do, what will make your blog stand out from all of the other blogs that your teacher has to read and grade?

The Missing Link

From pieces of art to armor, the Renaissance is the perfect period to find links to include in your blog that show everything you will be discussing within your weblog. Castles, kings, ladies, knights, painters, and writers can all be found on the Web and linked within your blog for others to discover.

ORDINARY

Leonardo da Vinci, Michelangelo, and Raphael are three of the artists most people think of when they think of the Renaissance period. Da Vinci's *Mona Lisa*, Michelangelo's *Pietá,* and Raphael's *The School of Athens* embody the artistic ideals of the high Renaissance.

EXTRAORDINARY

Leonardo da Vinci, Michelangelo, and Raphael are three of the artists most people think of when they think of the Renaissance period. Da Vinci's *Mona Lisa* (**http://www.artchive.com /artchive/L/leonardo/monalisa.jpg.html**), Michelangelo's *Pietá* (**http://www.artchive.com/ artchive/M/michelangelo/pieta.jpg.html**), and Raphael's *The School of Athens* (**http:// www.artchive.com/artchive/R/raphael/school _athens.jpg.html**) embody the artistic ideals of the high Renaissance.

Just discussing the artworks may fulfill the requirements of your assignment, but actually **posting links** to pictures of them in your blog **allows readers to click and see what you are talking about.**

TIP FILE

If one link is good, are more better? That depends. Adding a couple of extra good links to impress your teacher is probably a good idea. But just putting in any old link—especially dead ones!—is never a great idea.

Science

Science doesn't always take place in a lab. Sharing ideas and discussing theories are often just what a scientist needs to help inspire the next great discovery. And **what better place to share ideas with lots of like-minded scientists than on your very own blog?**

ASSIGNMENT 1

NEANDERTHALS AND MODERN HOMO SAPIENS

There are two main theories regarding Neanderthals and modern Homo sapiens. In a closed weblog, outline the two theories and discuss your beliefs regarding each group. Then examine the physical features and day-to-day lives of the Neanderthals. In subsequent entries, compare the lives of Neanderthals and modern Homo sapiens.

ASSIGNMENT 2

Dinosaurs ruled the land during three important geologic periods: the Triassic, Jurassic, and Cretaceous periods. Create a weblog in which you:

1. **Discuss at least four important aspects of each period.**

2. **Conclude with your hypothesis that explains why all the dinosaurs died.**

Triassic
Jurassic
Cretaceous

Creating Web pages (such as your blog) is a visual art. And **the way you put your words on the page is either going to invite people in to find out more or make them run in search of a more user-friendly page.**

ORDINARY

Modern Homo sapiens live in a world of conveniences. Those conveniences include indoor plumbing, grocery stores, refrigerators, stoves, ready-to-wear clothing, automobiles, telephones, and many other things. Neanderthals can be thought of as living in a world of inconvenience. They had to kill their own food (often at great risk to themselves) and cook it over open fires. Starting fires was no easy task without matches. And if there was leftover food, there was no place to store it. All of the technology that has led to the convenient lifestyle of modern humans had to be created over thousands of years.

Now let's take a look at the same information in a list format. It's easier to read and will probably invite more responses (in the form of additional list items) than the denser paragraph format. And the picture makes it all a bit more fun!

EXTRAORDINARY

Did you ever consider the many ways we modern humans have it easy compared to prehistoric people? Here are just a few of the conveniences that we take for granted, along with their Neanderthal counterparts.

Modern Homo sapiens	Neanderthals
Buy food at grocery stores	Killed animals for meat, picked wild fruits and vegetables
Shop at clothing stores	Skinned animals for their furs to keep warm
Store food in refrigerators	Ate food whenever they found it (they were always hungry!)
Stay warm using furnaces	Huddled around open fires to keep warm
Drive automobiles	Used feet

ASSIGNMENT 3

POLLUTION

In today's world, pollution is a topic that often appears in the news. Pollutants come in many forms—asbestos, oil spills, industrial waste, and pesticides. Research a few of these and really think about the effects these pollutants will have on future generations. Get passionate about your beliefs and let your weblog show it!

Find an online article about a pollution problem and provide the link to it on your weblog. Ask bloggers to come up with solutions to the pollution problems that plague our world. Encourage fellow bloggers to provide links to additional articles on the topic.

ASSIGNMENT 4

MARS

Mars has always fascinated humans. We may be able to send robotic devices that transmit pictures to the planet, but a manned mission seems an impossibility. Research the elements of travel to Mars that preclude us from actually getting there now. Is it transportation? The temperature of the planet? Find facts and then create a weblog where you discuss with bloggers what would be needed to safely travel and set up a space station on Mars.

TIP FILE

There is a world of online publications with great photos of our solar system. NASA (the National Aeronautics and Space Administration) also publishes pictures on the Web. To show the planet Mars on your blog, drop a picture or two into the posting or provide a link to relevant scientific sites.

PROJECT JUMP START

⭐ **Having trouble coming up with a topic or figuring** out how to make your blog different from everyone else's? Why not base your blog on a TV show? Here's an example:

⭐ **CSI: Crime Scene Investigation** took the television world and our imaginations by storm. Scientists use forensics every day to re-create the past and solve crimes. Find a newspaper article online about a crime. Post the link to the article so other bloggers can read it. In your postings, answer these questions:

- **What evidence would you look for at the scene?**

- **What evidence do you think you would find at the scene? What would you do with it?**

- **What people would I want to talk to about the crime?**

- **How important are CSI labs, with all their technology, in solving crimes?** Take a stance and support it in your blog. Open the discussion up to other bloggers.

BRAIN JAM:
Giving Your Readers a Voice

Have you ever gone online and read surveys? Isn't it fun to point, click and vote and then compare your opinion to others? You can do the same thing for your readers. Create a survey for your blog that others can take. It can give you valuable feedback on your blog, such as what readers do and do not like, what they would like to see more or less of, and other elements they'd like to see in your publication.

ezine

fluid

issues

content

static

is

politic

fluid

features

CHAPTER 6

EZINES

Hitting Newsstands Now

Hitting Newsstands Now

Now it's your turn to create an ezine. Remember: an ezine is an online magazine. **The most significant difference between an ezine and a Web site is that an ezine has fluid content and stories, whereas a Web site remains virtually static.** These assignments will have you creating online magazines, with articles, stories, and artwork within three categories: history, science, and English.

History Assignment

Create an ezine based on a major period of history, written as if you are living during that time. Some ideas include:

Ancient Greece	The American West
Medieval England	English Colonialism
The Renaissance	World War I
The Crusades	The Roaring Twenties
Colonial America	The Great Depression
Baroque Europe	World War II
The American Revolution	The Korean War
The Civil War	The Vietnam War

. . . or any other topic you think of or your teacher assigns!

Your ezine must include a title. Typically, the Web address is the name of the publication. You don't buy a "no-name" magazine at the newsstand, and your readers won't even find your ezine without a Web address.

Once you have a title, you must decide on content. Content in most ezines includes stories, features, pictures (graphics), information, profiles, and even advertisements. Remember—all this content must change.

Your ezine assignment must include THREE issues of the publication. Each issue must include:

- **Three stories on the major events during the period** (Please, no anachronisms; don't put a cell phone in an event that occurred fifty years ago. Stick to the correct timeline.)

- **Two stories on arts, culture, or artifacts** of the period you are covering

- **Two features on important people** of the period

- **Several graphics** corresponding to your content

- **Two advertisements** (What would be sold during this time period? Keep it authentic.)

These are the basics. Go for it! Have fun, get creative, be extraordinary, and learn all about another era.

Remember what you read earlier about the importance of creating intriguing and attention-grabbing titles? Imagine that you are coming up with titles for ezines about the following topics. What are some possibilities that come to mind?

- **horseback riding**
- **movie soundtracks**
- **skateboards and in-line skating**
- **school**
- **cooking**

Science Assignment

Ah—the world of discovery! Sciences offer us a look at how things work—everything from marine animals to the world's rotation. You will create an ezine based on a scientific topic. Some ideas include:

Astronomy and Our Solar System

The Human Body and Physiology

Endangered Species

Forensic Science (Crime Scene Investigation)

Meteorology

Natural Disasters (Hurricanes, Tsunamis, Earthquakes)

Physical and Cultural Anthropology

Psychology and Psychiatry

Physics

Zoology

Fossils

Health and Safety

Diseases and Disorders

Marine Biology

. . . or any other topic you think of or that your teacher assigns!

Your assignment is to come up with a title and publish three issues of your ezine. **Each issue must include the following components:**

- **One background story** providing general information on the subject

- **Three stories concerning recent advances or events** related to the subject you are covering

- **Two short (approximately three hundred word) features on facts** about the subject

- **Two features on important people** in the field of study

- **Several graphics** corresponding to your content

"Weblogs are known as the indie rock of the Internet; thousands of teens claim one for their own. They need no corporate might to sponsor their musing, doodles, or homework, and they need no permission to publish."

—Elizabeth Armstrong "Do You Blog?", published in the *Christian Science Monitor* online

Literature Assignment

You will create an ezine based on a major novel or play, written as if you are an observer within the novel's world, living in the same setting as the characters. Some possible works include:

Of Mice and Men	*The Great Gatsby*
Romeo and Juliet	*The Catcher in the Rye*
The Odyssey	*Where the Red Fern Grows*
To Kill a Mockingbird	*A Raisin in the Sun*
1984	*Huckleberry Finn*
Into the Wild	*Oliver Twist*
Lord of the Flies	*Our Town*
Night	*Othello*
All Quiet on the Western Front	*A Farewell to Arms*
	Dune

Your ezine must include a title. You will publish three issues, and each issue must include:

- **A plot summary:** you decide how much of the literary work to include within each issue of your ezine

- **Three stories related to the symbolism** within the chapters or acts you are covering within each issue

- **Two stories on themes** within the literary work

- **Two features on important people** of the period

- **Two features on characters** within the literary work and their pertinence to the story line; write the story as if it is a personality profile you'd find in a publication

- **Several graphics** corresponding to your content

These are the basics. Think of different categories that you might want to cover. For example, in *Lord of the Flies,* there are several Biblical references and symbols. You might include a "segment" button on Biblical symbolism and include your stories on symbolism within that design element. Have fun and create something amazing. Engross yourself in the fictitious world of extraordinary characters.

"In my experience, what makes a blog cool or not is content and content alone. All the other stuff you mention is 'nice to have' bells and whistles. A blog can have every technological feature in the world but without content it is nothing."

—Blogger Vincent O'Sullivan, in a posting on *Metablog: A Blog About Blogging*

Modern Times

One last note about high-tech assignment options.
Just as blogs are the Web-based versions of journals
and ezines are the electronic versions of magazines,
there is a Web-based version of a radio broadcast. **A**
***podcast* is "a non-music audio broadcast that has
been converted to an MP3 file or other audio file
format for playback in a digital music player."** It
is sometimes called "blogcasting," "audio magazine,"
or "audioblogging" since an iPod is not needed. It
can be news, sports, or talk and is available through
subscription services. Through podcasting, independent
companies can create their own individual shows, and
established radio and TV programs can distribute their
information in a new format.

Podcasting is growing at an unprecedented rate. On
Google, the term got 24 hits on September 28, 2004. As
of November 5, 2005, Google was reporting 90,100,000
hits. Today, podcasting is used for:

- **education**

- **politics**

- **religion**

- **unofficial audio tours of public places**

- **television commentary**

- **conferences and meeting alerts
  within a company**

- **advocacy for issues**

- **youth media**

In 2005, a communications course at the University of
Western Australia used student-created podcasts as the
main assessment item for the class. It may be coming
to your classroom soon!

RESOURCES:

To find out more about podcasting, check out these sites:

http://www.podcast411.com/page2.html

http://ipodder.sourceforge.net/index.php

"In the end, if MP3 players become so ubiquitous that we are invaded by ear-bud-wearing podcasting people, they will probably be too pre-occupied with choosing from all these programming options to screech and point at those not connected to the mothership."

—Christine Boese, "Invasion of the Podcasting People?", CNN Headline News Online, 12-08-04

Heads Up!

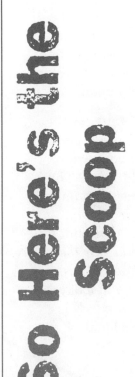

So Here's the Scoop

Learning the lingo is important so here is a pod primer for you:

mobilecasting: podcasting to mobile phones

palmcasting: podcasting to Palm devices

photofeed: image podcasting

podcatcher: the client program that captures the audio feed and synchronizes it with the music player

podshanking: transferring music files directly from one iPod to another. First-generation Podshanking uses a cable from the headphones jack of the source iPod to a voice recorder accessory on the destination iPod.

podzilla: a popular gadget bag for portable music players, PDAs, and the like

vidcasting/vodcasting: two names for voice-based podcasts

PROJECT JUMP START

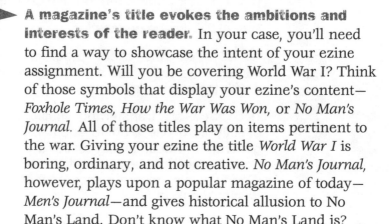

★ **Think about the titles of your favorite magazines and online sites.** What do they have in common? They probably all describe the interests of the people who read the magazine. *Bike* magazine, for example, covers topics of interest to people who ride bikes. *Seventeen* magazine covers stories of interest to teenage girls seventeen years of age and under.

★ **A magazine's title evokes the ambitions and interests of the reader.** In your case, you'll need to find a way to showcase the intent of your ezine assignment. Will you be covering World War I? Think of those symbols that display your ezine's content— *Foxhole Times, How the War Was Won,* or *No Man's Journal.* All of those titles play on items pertinent to the war. Giving your ezine the title *World War I* is boring, ordinary, and not creative. *No Man's Journal,* however, plays upon a popular magazine of today— *Men's Journal*—and gives historical allusion to No Man's Land. Don't know what No Man's Land is? Look it up!

BRAIN JAM:
Who Are You?

Christopher Knight, an ezine expert who writes regularly for emailuniverse.com, writes about the importance of filling your ezine with your distinct personality. He says, "Every print magazine that you pick up has a personality to it. You instinctively know the 'feeling' it delivers."

Make sure that your readers know who YOU are— tell them about you, let them know your connection to the ezine. Why are you doing it? (and don't just say to get a good grade and pass the class). Why did you select this topic? What is your position on it? Readers will relate much better to an ezine if they know just who is behind it.

As Knight puts it, "Be unique. There must be something that you do, say, have passion for, or some way to differentitate your personality from the noise of the ezine marketplace."

TO FIND OUT MORE

Books

Blood, Rebecca. *The Weblog Handbook: Practical Advice on Creating and Maintaining Your Blog.* Cambridge, MA: Perseus Publishing, 2002.

Gill, Martha. *Webworks: E-zines: Explore On-line Magazine Design.* Gloucester, MA: Rockport Publishers, 2000.

McFedries, Paul. *The Complete Idiot's Guide to Creating a Web Page and Blog.* Indianapolis: Alpha, 2004.

Niederst, Jennifer. *Web Design in a Nutshell.* Sebastopol, CA: O'Reilly, 2001.

Slocombe, Mike. *Max Hits: Building and Promoting Successful Web Sites.* Gloucester, MA: Rotovision, 2002.

Stone, Biz. *Blogging: Genius Strategies for Instant Web Content.* Indianapolis: New Riders Publishing, 2002.

Stone, Biz. *Who Let the Blogs Out?: A Hyperconnected Peek at the World of Weblogs.* New York: St. Martin's Griffin, 2004.

Organizations and Online Sites

Blogs 101
http://www.nytimes.com/ref/technology/blogs_101.html
This *New York Times* site showcases some of the most popular blogs in diverse categories and asks bloggers to provide their picks for the most popular sites.

CNET.com The Power of 10
http://www.cnet.com/4520-11136_1-6268155-1.html
Have fun at this site, which takes a look at the top ten Web fads. The ninth entry? Blogging, of course.

The Fifth Annual Weblog Awards
http://2005.bloggies.com
Blogs and ezines are such a part of the popular culture that there are weblog awards—The Bloggies. Check out this site to see the categories of blogs and entries for the fifth annual awards.

Figuring Out Blogs and Whatever s Next
http://www.sreetips.com/blogs.html
This site offers workshops and other information to get you actively involved in the blogosphere.

Internet Public Library for Teens Teen Space
http://www.ipl.org/div/teen/browse/rw0000/
This site contains lots of information on reading and writing, including fun reading lists and links to ezines and blogs.

lovetoknowTOP10
http://www.lovetoknow.com/top10/blogs.html
This site provides a list of the top ten blogs as selected by the site's editors. There are also links to other popular blog sites on numerous subjects.

My Favorite Ezines
http://www.myfavoriteezines.com

This site is one of the most popular ezine and online newsletter directories. Scan these educational, inspirational, motivational, and recreational sites to get ideas and to gather information and research.

NVU
http://www.nvu.com

This site offers a free program that will guide you in the programming of a Web site (or ezine).

Technorati
http://www.technorati.com/pop/blogs

This site contains links to blogs on many different topics. No matter what you want to read about and blog about, you'll find it on this organized, easy-to-use site.

INDEX

Abbreviations, 26, 27, 31
About.com, 50
acronyms, 26, 27
Allure magazine, 60
American Booksellers
    Foundation For Free
    Expression, 75
American Journalism Review,
    51
archives, 21, 26
Arial font, 69
audiences, 11, 24, 51, 59
"audio magazines," 117
"audioblogging," 117

Bike magazine, 120
black-and-white photography,
    72
"blogcasting," 117
"Blogging 101: Hosting Your
    Own Blog" article, 48
Blogging for Teens (John W.
    Gosney), 26
blogging software, 19, 47, 53,
    68, 81
blogosphere, 21, 31, 42
blogs
    abbreviations, 26, 27, 31
    acronyms, 26, 27
    archives, 21, 26
    article synopses, 92
    athletes and, 24
    audiences, 11, 24, 51
    celebrities and, 24
    closed blogs, 49
    concluding paragraphs, 37,
        39, 97
    diaries compared to, 25
    domain names, 46, 48
    format, 102–103
    freedom of speech and, 75
    freedom of the press and,
        75
    grammatical usage of, 18
    graphics in, 86, 88–89, 105
    history class and, 94–99
    hosting services, 44,
        46–47, 49, 52
    instant messages (IMs)
        compared to, 20, 22
    introductory postings, 37,
        38, 40, 41, 43, 81, 87, 95,
        97
    journals compared to, 25
    language in, 45
    libel and, 74
    links in, 21, 98, 99, 104
    locating, 15
    moderated blogs, 49
    open blogs, 49
    open source programs, 68
    personal blogs, 17, 27, 42,
        43, 44, 46
    personal information in,
        70
    planning, 34–35
    posting dates, 42
    postings, 23, 34, 36, 37, 39,
        40, 41, 42, 43, 49, 81
    premium hosting services,
        46, 47
    quotes in, 37, 38, 39, 81, 96
    registration, 48
    requests for posts, 34, 36,
        43, 90, 93, 97, 104
    responses, 29
    September 11 attacks and,
        16
    software, 19, 47, 53, 68, 81
    surveys in, 121
    templates, 35, 37–39, 49

titles, 34, 36, 40, 43, 47, 81, 82–83, 87, 95, 97
tone, 16, 27
topical blogs, 17, 23
topics, 14, 23, 27, 34, 81, 90, 91, 106
writer's block, 50
blogstorms, 21
Blood, Rebecca, 46–47
Boese, Christine, 118

Car and Driver magazine, 60
Christian Science Monitor, 114
clip art, 72, 73
closed blogs, 49
CNN Headline News Online, 118
color photography, 72
computers, 10
copyright restrictions, 71, 73
CSI: Crime Scene Investigation Las Vegas (television show), 106
current events, 17, 63, 90, 91, 94

Demographics, 59, 61, 62
diaries, 25, 26
"Do You Blog?" (Elizabeth Armstrong), 114
domain names, 46, 48

Educational standards, 6, 7, 8, 80
email, 16, 26, 31, 50, 56, 77
ezines
    action photos, 72, 76
    audiences, 59
    captions, 71
    colors, 70–71
    content, 63, 66, 67, 73
    copyright restrictions and, 71, 73
    demographics, 61
    editors, 61
    facts, 74
    fluid content of, 57–58, 110

font sizes, 69, 76
fonts, 67, 69, 76
freedom of speech, 75
freedom of the press, 75
graphics, 71–72, 73, 111, 113, 115
guest editorials, 77
headlines, 73
history class and, 110–112
hosting services, 66
illustrations, 76
interviews, 77
layout, 67, 73, 76
libel and, 74
line spacing, 69
links to, 58
literature class and, 115–116
marketing, 56
niche audiences, 59
personal information in, 70
personality of, 107
responses, 29
search engines and, 56, 60
software, 68
subscriptions, 56
templates, 66, 70
theme, 66, 70
titles, 111, 112, 115, 120
tone, 72
Web sites compared to, 57, 110

Fees, 46
First Amendment, 75
foreshadowing, 87
forums, 14, 24, 47

Grading rules. See rubrics.

Hosting services, 52, 66

Instant messages (IMs), 16, 19, 20, 21, 22, 26, 31
Internet, 6, 7, 11, 14, 16, 20

introductory postings, 37, 38, 40, 41, 43, 81, 87, 95, 97

Language arts, 80–93
Lee, Harper, 84
legal counsel, 74
libel, 74
libraries, 10
links, 21, 98, 99, 104

Metablog: A Blog About Blogging, 116
metaphors, 87
mobilecasting, 119
moderated blogs, 49
MP3 files, 117
MSNBC, 16
MySpace.com, 53

Names. See titles.
NASA (National Aeronautics and Space Adminstration), 105
National Council of Teachers of English (NCTE), 8
Network Solutions, 48
New Yorker magazine, 67

Open blogs, 49
open source programs, 68

Palmcasting, 119
permalinks, 20
personal blogs, 17, 27, 42, 43, 44, 46
photofeed, 119
podcasts, 117, 118–119
podcatchers, 119
podshanking, 119
podzilla, 119
pollution, 104
pop-up ads, 46
portfolios, 90

postings, 23, 34, 36, 37, 39, 40, 41, 42, 43, 49, 81
premium hosting services, 46, 47

Redbook magazine, 60
registration services, 48
rubrics, 9

San Jose Mercury News, 16
search engines, 10, 15, 56, 60
September 11 attacks, 16
Seventeen magazine, 60, 120
similes, 87
software, 19, 47, 53, 68, 81
symbolism, 84–85, 87

Templates, 35, 37–39, 49, 66, 70
themes. See topics.
Time magazine, 66
titles, 34, 36, 38, 40, 43
To Kill a Mockingbird (Harper Lee), 84
tone, 16, 27, 72
topical blogs, 17, 23
topics, 14, 23, 27, 28, 34, 81, 90, 91, 106

U.S. Constitution, 75
user forums, 47

Vidcasting, 119
vodcasting, 119

Web sites, 8, 10, 15, 24, 35, 47, 48, 53, 57, 58, 66, 67, 72, 75, 99, 102, 110
The Weblog Handbook: Practical Advice on Creating and Maintaining Your Blog (Rebecca Blood), 46
weblogs. See blogs.

LYNNE ROMINGER

Lynne Rominger is an educator and journalist residing in Northern California with her husband and four children—all fluent in the inner workings of the Internet. She occasionally blogs and often writes content for ezines, among other publications. Rominger is the author of more than three hundred articles and six books, two on writing, two on teaching, one cookbook, and one collection of military essays. She is currently working on her eighth title, *Budget Beauty: How to Look Like a Princess on a Pauper's Pocketbook* (Adams Media). When not writing, Rominger enjoys looking for seashells on the seashore. Incidentally, the last sentence included alliteration, a common literary device.